Keto Chaffle Recipes Cookbook for Beginners

Simple, Easy and Irresistible Low Carb
and Gluten Free Ketogenic Waffle Recipes
to Lose Weight, Reverse Disease, Boost
Brain and Live Healthy

Irma Baker

Table of Contents

Introduction

A chaffle is a waffle but made with a cheese base. Basically, it's shredded cheese and an egg mixture. Sometimes for fluffier recipes, it's a cream cheese instead of shredded cheese. It's the trendy new keto-friendly recipe because it's low in carbs, and it base won't spike your insulin levels, causing fat storage.

A low carb, keto-friendly, sugar-free food kind of ticks all of the boxes when you're aiming to lower your carbohydrate intake.

For a sweet chaffle, some usual ingredients you'll find are mozzarella cheese, egg, cinnamon, almond flour, vanilla, and low carb sweeteners like allulose or swerve.

In savory chaffles, mozzarella can be used, but sharper, saltier cheeses like cheddar or Colby jack are often mixed with ingredients like garlic powder, everything bagel seasoning, onion, Jalapenos, etc. The combinations are really endless for both sweet and savory versions.

In this book, you'll learn how to prepare over 50 Keto Chaffle Recipes and their variations, their nutritional values, waffle maker to use for keto chaffle, chaffle sweeteners, how to grill and freeze chaffles and lots more.

This book also contains pictures of the different recipes to give you an illustration of how the various recipes looks like after making them. Keep reading, keep practicing keto chaffle, and keep living a healthier life!

Happy reading!

Keto Chaffle Recipes Variations

Basic Keto Chaffle Recipe

Prep Time: 5 mins

Cook Time: 8 mins

Servings: 1

Ingredients:

- 1 egg
- 1/2 cup cheddar cheese, shredded

Instructions:

- Turn waffle maker on or plug it in so that it heats and grease both sides.

- In a small bowl, crack an egg, then add the 1/2 cup cheddar cheese and stir to combine.
- Pour 1/2 of the batter in the waffle maker and close the top.
- Cook for 3-4 minutes or until it reaches desired doneness.
- Carefully remove from waffle maker and set aside for 2-3 minutes to give it time to crisp.
- Follow the instructions again to make the second chaffle.

Nutritional Value (per serving):

- Calories: 291kcal
- Carbohydrates: 1g
- Protein: 20g
- Fat: 23g
- Saturated Fat: 13g
- Cholesterol: 223mg
- Sodium: 413mg
- Potassium: 116mg
- Sugar: 1g
- Vitamin A: 804IU
- Calcium: 432mg
- Iron: 1mg

Variations to the Basic Keto Chaffle Recipe:

- Experiment with different kinds of cheese such as Monterrey Jack, Colby, mozzarella cheese, etc. You could even combine two different kinds of cheese for added flavor.

- Add spices such as garlic powder, Italian seasoning, Everything But the Bagel seasoning, or red pepper flakes to turn it up a notch
- Add a tsp of coconut flour or a tablespoon of almond flour along with 1/4 tsp baking powder and a pinch of salt.
- Thinly chopped peppers, onions, or jalapenos can add flavor and texture.
- Keep it sugar-free by adding keto-friendly sweeteners like Lakanto Monkfruit or Swerve to make a sweet Chaffle.

Chocolate Chip Chaffle Keto Recipe

Prep Time: 5 mins

Cook Time: 8 mins

Serving: 1

Ingredients:

- 1 egg
- 1 tbsp heavy whipping cream
- 1/2 tsp coconut flour
- 1 3/4 tsp Lakanto monk fruit golden can use more or less to adjust sweetness
- 1/4 tsp baking powder
- pinch of salt
- 1 tbsp Lily's Chocolate Chips

Instructions:

- Turn on the waffle maker so that it heats up.
- In a small bowl, combine all ingredients except the chocolate chips and stir well until combined.
- Grease waffle maker, then pour half of the batter onto the bottom plate of the waffle maker. Sprinkle a few chocolate chips on top and then close.
- Cook for 3-4 minutes or until the chocolate chip chaffle dessert is golden brown, then remove from waffle maker with a fork, being careful not to burn your fingers.
- Repeat with the rest of the batter.
- Let chaffle sit for a few minutes so that it begins to crisp. If desired, serve with sugar-free whipped topping.

Nutritional Value (per serving):

- Calories: 146kcal
- Carbohydrates: 7g
- Protein: 6g
- Fat: 10g
- Saturated Fat: 7g
- Fiber: 3g
- Sugar: 1g

Keto Blueberry Chaffle

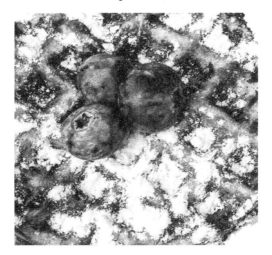

Prep Time: 3 minutes

Cook Time: 15 minutes

Servings: 5

Ingredients:

- 1 cup of mozzarella cheese
- 2 tablespoons almond flour
- 1 tsp baking powder
- 2 eggs
- 1 tsp cinnamon
- 2 tsp of Swerve
- 3 tablespoon blueberries

Instructions:

- Heat up your Dash mini waffle maker.
- In a mixing bowl, add the mozzarella cheese, almond flour, baking powder, eggs, cinnamon, swerve, and blueberries. Mix well, so all the ingredients are mixed together.
- Spray your mini waffle maker with nonstick cooking spray.
- Add in a little bit less than 1/4 a cup of blueberry keto waffle batter.
- Close the lid and cook the chaffle for 3-5 minutes. Check it at the 3-minute mark to see if it is crispy and brown. If it is not or it sticks to the top of the waffle machine, close the lid and cook for 1-2 minutes longer.
- Serve with a sprinkle of swerve confectioners sugar or keto syrup.

Nutritional Value (per serving):

- Calories: 116kcal
- Carbohydrates: 3g
- Protein: 8g

- Fat: 8g
- Saturated Fat: 4g
- Cholesterol: 83mg
- Sodium: 166mg
- Potassium: 142mg
- Fiber: 1g
- Sugar: 1g
- Vitamin A: 246IU
- Vitamin C: 1mg
- Calcium: 177mg
- Iron: 1mg

Cinnamon Roll Keto Chaffles

Prep Time: 5 minutes

Cook Time: 10 minutes

Servings: 3

Ingredients:

Cinnamon Roll Chaffle Ingredients:

- 1/2 cup mozzarella cheese
- 1 tablespoon almond flour
- 1/4 tsp baking powder
- 1 egg
- 1 tsp cinnamon
- 1 tsp Granulated Swerve

Cinnamon roll swirl Ingredients:

- 1 tbsp butter
- 1 tsp cinnamon
- 2 tsp confectioners swerve
- Keto Cinnamon Roll Glaze
- 1 tablespoon butter
- 1 tablespoon cream cheese
- 1/4 tsp vanilla extract
- 2 tsp swerve confectioners

Instructions:

- Plug in your Mini Dash Waffle maker and let it heat up.
- In a small bowl mix the mozzarella cheese, almond flour, baking powder, egg, 1 teaspoon cinnamon, and 1 teaspoon swerve granulated and set aside.
- In another small bowl, add a tablespoon of butter, 1 teaspoon cinnamon, and 2 teaspoons of swerve confectioners sweetener.
- Microwave for 15 seconds and mix well.

- Spray the waffle maker with nonstick spray and add 1/3 of the batter to your waffle maker. Swirl in 1/3 of the cinnamon, swerve, and butter mixture onto the top of it. Close the waffle maker and let cook for 3-4 minutes.
- When the first cinnamon roll chaffle is done, make the second and then make the third.
- While the third chaffle is cooking place 1 tablespoon butter and 1 tablespoon of cream cheese in a small bowl. Heat in the microwave for 10-15 seconds. Start at 10, and if the cream cheese is not soft enough to mix with the butter heat for an additional 5 seconds.
- Add the vanilla extract, and the swerve confectioners sweetener to the butter and cream cheese and mix well using a whisk.
- Drizzle keto cream cheese glaze on top of chaffle.

Nutritional Value (per serving):

- Calories: 180kcal
- Carbohydrates: 3g
- Protein: 7g
- Fat: 16g
- Saturated Fat: 9g
- Cholesterol: 95mg
- Sodium: 221mg
- Potassium: 77mg
- Fiber: 1g
- Sugar: 1g

- Vitamin A: 505IU
- Calcium: 148mg
- Iron: 1mg

Keto Chaffle Breakfast Sandwich

Prep Time: 3 minutes

Cook Time: 6 minutes

Servings: 1

Ingredients:

- 1 egg
- 1/2 cup Monterey Jack Cheese
- 1 tablespoon almond flour
- 2 tablespoons butter

Instructions:

- In a small bowl, mix the egg, almond flour, and Monterey Jack Cheese.
- Pour half of the batter into your mini waffle maker and cook for 3-4 minutes. Then cook the rest of the batter to make a second chaffle.
- In a small pan, melt 2 tablespoons of butter. Add the chaffles and cook on each side for 2 minutes. Pressing down while they are cooking lightly on the top of them, so they crisp up better.
- Remove from the pan and let sit for 2 minutes.

Nutritional Value (per serving):

- Calories: 514kcal
- Carbohydrates: 2g
- Protein: 21g
- Fat: 47g
- Saturated Fat: 27g
- Cholesterol: 274mg
- Sodium: 565mg
- Potassium: 106mg
- Fiber: 1g
- Sugar: 1g
- Vitamin A: 1372IU
- Calcium: 461mg
- Iron: 1mg

Keto Chaffle Taco Shells

Prep Time: 5 minutes

Cook Time: 20 minutes

Servings: 5

Ingredients:

- 1 tablespoon almond flour
- 1 cup taco blend cheese
- 2 eggs
- 1/4 tsp taco seasoning

Instructions:

- In a bowl, mix almond flour, taco blend cheese, eggs, and taco seasoning. I find it easiest to mix everything using a fork.
- Add 1.5 tablespoons of taco chaffle batter to the waffle maker at a time — Cook chaffle batter in the waffle maker for 4 minutes.
- Remove the taco chaffle shell from the waffle maker and drape over the side of a

bowl. I used my pie pan because it was what I had on hand, but just about any bowl will work.

- Continue making chaffle taco shells until you are out of batter. Then fill your taco shells with taco meat, your favorite toppings, and enjoy!

Nutritional Value (per serving):

- Calories: 113kcal
- Carbohydrates: 1g
- Protein: 8g
- Fat: 9g
- Saturated Fat: 4g
- Cholesterol: 87mg
- Sodium: 181mg
- Potassium: 43mg
- Fiber: 1g
- Sugar: 1g
- Vitamin A: 243IU
- Calcium: 160mg
- Iron: 1mg

Garlic Bread Chaffles

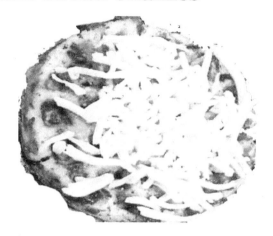

Prep Time: 3 minutes

Cook Time: 11 minutes

Servings: 2

Ingredients:

- 1/2 cup shredded Mozzarella cheese
- 1 egg
- 1/2 tsp basil
- 1/4 tsp garlic powder
- 1 tbsp almond flour
- 1 tbsp butter
- 1/4 tsp garlic powder
- 1/4 cup shredded mozzarella cheese

Instructions:

- Heat up your Dash mini waffle maker.
- In a small bowl, mix the egg, 1/2 tsp basil, 1/4 tsp garlic powder, 1 tablespoon

almond flour and 1/2 cup Mozzarella Cheese.

- Add 1/2 of the batter into your mini waffle maker and cook for 4 minutes. If they are still a bit uncooked, leave it cooking for another 2 minutes. Then cook the rest of the batter to make a second chaffle.
- In a small bowl, add 1 tablespoon butter and 1/4 tsp garlic powder and melt in the microwave. It will take about 25 seconds or so, depending on your microwave.
- Place the chaffles on a baking sheet and use a rubber brush to spread the butter and garlic mixture on top.
- Add 1/8th a cup of cheese on top of each chaffle.
- Put chaffles in the oven or a toaster oven at 400 degrees and cook until the cheese is melted.

Nutritional Value (per serving):

- Calories: 231kcal
- Carbohydrates: 2g
- Protein: 13g
- Fat: 19g
- Saturated Fat: 10g
- Cholesterol: 130mg
- Sodium: 346mg
- Potassium: 52mg
- Fiber: 1g
- Sugar: 1g
- Vitamin A: 580IU
- Calcium: 232mg

- Iron: 1mg

Peanut Butter Chaffle

Prep Time: 3 minutes

Cook Time: 8 minutes

Servings: 2

Ingredients:

- 1 egg
- 1/2 cup mozzarella cheese shredded
- 3 tablespoons swerve granulated
- 2 tbsp peanut butter

Instructions:

- Heat up your waffle maker.

- In a bowl, mix the peanut butter, egg, granulated swerve, and mozzarella cheese.
- Pour half of the chaffle batter into the waffle maker and cook for 4 minutes.
- Carefully remove once cooked and place on a plate to cool. The chaffle will be a little flimsy when you remove it, but it will stiffen up as it cools.
- Next, cook your second chaffle and let it sit for 2 minutes after you cook it.

Nutritional Value (per serving):

- Calories: 210kcal
- Carbohydrates: 4g
- Protein: 13g
- Fat: 16g
- Saturated Fat: 6g
- Cholesterol: 104mg
- Sodium: 280mg
- Potassium: 155mg
- Fiber: 1g
- Sugar: 2g
- Vitamin A: 308IU
- Calcium: 161mg
- Iron: 1mg

Pumpkin Chocolate Chip Chaffles

Prep Time: 4 minutes

Cook Time: 12 minutes

Servings: 3

Ingredients:

- 1/2 cup shredded mozzarella cheese
- 4 teaspoons pumpkin puree
- 1 egg
- 2 tablespoons granulated Swerve
- 1/4 tsp pumpkin pie spice
- 4 teaspoons sugar-free chocolate chips
- 1 tablespoon almond flour

Instructions:

- Plug in your waffle maker.

- In a small bowl, mix the pumpkin puree and egg. Make sure you mix it well, so all the pumpkin is mixed with the egg.
- Next, add in the mozzarella cheese, almond flour, swerve and add pumpkin spice and mix well.
- Then add in your sugar-free chocolate chips
- Add half the keto pumpkin pie Chaffle mix to the Dish Mini waffle maker at a time. Cook chaffle batter in the waffle maker for 4 minutes.
- Do not open before the 4 minutes is up. It is very important that you do not open the waffle maker before the 4-minute mark. After that you can open it to check it and make sure it is cooked all the way, but with these chaffles keeping the lid closed the whole time is very important.
- When the first one is completely done cooking cook the second one.
- Enjoy with some swerve confectioners sweetener or whipped cream on top.

Nutritional Value (per serving):

- Calories: 93kcal
- Carbohydrates: 2g
- Protein: 7g
- Fat: 7g
- Saturated Fat: 3g
- Cholesterol: 69mg
- Sodium: 138mg
- Potassium: 48mg

- Fiber: 1g
- Sugar: 1g
- Vitamin A: 1228IU
- Calcium: 107mg
- Iron: 1mg

Peanut Butter Chocolate Chip Chaffle

Prep Time: 2 minutes

Cook Time: 8 minutes

Servings: 2

Ingredients:

- 1 egg.
- 1/4 cup shredded mozzarella cheese

- 2 tablespoons creamy Peanut Butter.
- 1 tablespoon Almond Flour.
- 1 tablespoon Granulated Swerve.
- 1 teaspoon Vanilla extract.
- 1 tablespoon low carb chocolate chips.

Instructions:

- Plug in your waffle maker.
- In a small bowl, mix the peanut butter and egg. Make sure you mix it well, so all the peanut butter is mixed with the egg.
- Next, add in the mozzarella cheese, almond flour, swerve and chocolate chips and mix well.
- Add half the keto peanut butter chocolate chip Chaffle mix to the Dish Mini waffle maker at a time. Cook chaffle batter in the waffle maker for 4 minutes.
- When the first one is completely done cooking cook the second one.
- Enjoy with some swerve confectioners sweetener or whipped cream on top.

Nutritional Value (per serving):

- Calories: 193kcal
- Carbohydrates: 5g
- Protein: 11g
- Fat: 15g
- Saturated Fat: 4g
- Cholesterol: 93mg
- Sodium: 193mg
- Potassium: 134mg

- Fiber: 1g
- Sugar: 2g
- Vitamin A: 213IU
- Calcium: 97mg
- Iron: 1mg

Broccoli & Cheese Chaffle

Prep Time: 2 minutes

Cook Time: 8 minutes

Servings: 2

Ingredients:

- 1/2 cup cheddar cheese
- 1/4 cup fresh chopped broccoli
- 1 egg
- 1/4 teaspoon garlic powder
- 1 tablespoon almond flour

Instructions:

- In a bowl, mix almond flour, cheddar cheese, egg, and garlic powder. I find it easiest to mix everything using a fork.
- Add half the Broccoli and Cheese Chaffle batter to the Dish Mini waffle maker at a time.
- Cook chaffle batter in the waffle maker for 4 minutes.
- Let each chaffle sit for 1-2 minutes on a plate to firm up. Enjoy alone or dipping in sour cream or ranch dressing.

Nutritional Value (per serving):

- Calories: 170kcal
- Carbohydrates: 2g
- Protein: 11g
- Fat: 13g
- Saturated Fat: 7g
- Cholesterol: 112mg
- Sodium: 211mg
- Potassium: 94mg
- Fiber: 1g
- Sugar: 1g
- Vitamin A: 473IU
- Vitamin C: 10mg
- Calcium: 229mg
- Iron: 1mg

French Dip Keto Chaffle Sandwich

Prep Time: 5 mins

Cook Time: 12 mins

Servings: 2

Ingredients:

- 1 egg white
- 1/4 cup mozzarella cheese, shredded (packed)
- 1/4 cup sharp cheddar cheese, shredded (packed)
- 3/4 tsp water
- 1 tsp coconut flour
- 1/4 tsp baking powder
- Pinch of salt

Instructions:

- Preheat oven to 425 degrees. Plug the Dash Mini Waffle Maker in the wall and grease lightly once it is hot.
- Combine all of the ingredients in a bowl and stir to combine.
- Spoon out 1/2 of the batter on the waffle maker and close lid. Set a timer for 4 minutes and do not lift the lid until the cooking time is complete. Lifting beforehand can cause the Chaffle keto sandwich recipe to separate and stick to the waffle iron. You have to let it cook the entire 4 minutes before lifting the lid.
- Remove the chaffle from the waffle iron and set aside. Repeat the same steps above with the rest of the chaffle batter.
- Cover a cookie sheet with parchment paper and place chaffles a few inches apart.
- Add 1/4 to 1/3 cup of the slow cooker keto roast beef from the following recipe. Make sure to drain the excess broth/gravy before adding to the top of the chaffle.
- Add a slice of deli cheese or shredded cheese on top. Swiss and provolone are both great options.
- Place on the top rack of the oven for 5 minutes so that the cheese can melt. If you'd like the cheese to bubble and begin to brown, turn oven to broil for 1 min. (The swiss cheese may not brown)
- Enjoy open-faced with a small bowl of beef broth for dipping.

Note:

The nutritional information provided is only for the chaffles sandwich keto recipe. It does not include the beef or added cheese on top of the sandwich. That info will vary depending on the cut of beef you use and type of cheese.

Nutritional Value (per serving):

- Calories: 118kcal
- Carbohydrates: 2g
- Protein: 9g
- Fat: 8g
- Fiber: 1g

Fudgy Chocolate Chaffles

Prep Time: 5 mins

Cook Time: 8 mins

Servings: 2

Ingredients:

- 1 egg
- 2 tbsp mozzarella cheese, shredded
- 2 tbsp cocoa
- 2 tbsp Lakanto monk fruit powdered
- 1 tsp coconut flour
- 1 tsp heavy whipping cream
- 1/4 tsp baking powder
- 1/4 tsp vanilla extract
- pinch of salt

Instructions:

- Turn on waffle or chaffle maker. I use the Dash Mini Waffle Maker. Grease lightly or use a cooking spray.
- In a small bowl, combine all ingredients.
- Cover the dash mini waffle maker with 1/2 of the batter. Close the mini waffle maker and cook for 4 minutes. Remove the chaffle from the waffle maker carefully as it is very hot.
- Repeat the steps above.
- Serve with sugar-free strawberry ice cream or sugar-free whipped topping.

Note:

- The nutritional information does not include the Lakanto Monkfruit powdered sugar as most subtract to calculate net carbs. The nutritional info is based on one chaffle per serving.

- The nutritional information is provided for the fudgy chocolate chaffle recipe only.

Nutritional Value (per serving):

- Calories: 109kcal
- Carbohydrates: 5g
- Protein: 7g
- Fat: 7g
- Saturated Fat: 4g
- Cholesterol: 97mg
- Sodium: 132mg
- Potassium: 176mg
- Fiber: 3g
- Sugar: 1g
- Vitamin A: 255IU
- Calcium: 121mg
- Iron: 1mg

Keto Cornbread Chaffle

Ingredients:

- 1 egg

- 1/2 cup cheddar cheese shredded (or mozzarella)
- 5 slices jalapeno optional - picked or fresh
- 1 tsp Frank's Red hot sauce
- 1/4 tsp corn extract
- pinch salt

Instructions:

- Preheat the mini waffle maker
- In a small bowl, whip the egg.
- Add the remaining ingredients and mix it until it's well incorporated.
- Add a teaspoon of shredded cheese to the waffle maker for 30 seconds before adding the mixture. This will create a nice and crisp crust that is absolutely fantastic!
- Add half the mixture to the preheated waffle maker.
- Cook it for a minimum of 3 to 4 minutes. The longer you cook it, the crispier it gets.
- Serve warm and enjoy!

Keto Chaffle Stuffing Recipe

Servings: 4

Ingredients:

Basic Chaffle ingredients:

- 1/2 cup cheese mozzarella, cheddar or a combo of both
- 2 eggs
- 1/4 tsp garlic powder
- 1/2 tsp onion powder
- 1/2 tsp dried poultry seasoning
- 1/4 tsp salt
- 1/4 tsp pepper

Stuffing ingredients:

- 1 small onion diced
- 2 celery stalks
- 4 oz mushrooms diced
- 4 tbs butter for sauteing
- 3 eggs

Instructions:

- First, make your chaffles.
- Preheat the mini waffle iron.
- Preheat the oven to 350F
- In a medium-size bowl, combine the chaffle ingredients.
- Pour a 1/4 of the mixture into a mini waffle maker and cook each chaffle for about 4 minutes each.
- Once they are all cooked, set them aside.
- In a small frying pan, saute the onion, celery, and mushrooms until they are soft.
- In a separate bowl, tear up the chaffles into small pieces, add the sauteed veggies, and 3 eggs. Mix until the ingredients are fully combined.
- Add the stuffing mixture to a small casserole dish (about a 4 x 4) and bake it at 350 degrees for about 30 to 40 minutes.

Banana Nut Chaffle Recipe

Servings: 2

Ingredients:

- 1 egg
- 1 tbs cream cheese, softened and room temp
- 1 tbs sugar-free cheesecake pudding optional ingredient because it is dirty keto
- 1/2 cup mozzarella cheese
- 1 tbs Monkfruit confectioners
- 1/4 tsp vanilla extract
- 1/4 tsp banana extract

Optional Toppings:

- Sugar-free caramel sauce
- Pecans

Instructions:

- Preheat the mini waffle maker
- In a small bowl, whip the egg.

34

- Add the remaining ingredients to the egg mixture and mix it until it's well incorporated.
- Add half the batter to the waffle maker and cook it for a minimum of 4 minutes until it's golden brown.
- Remove the finished chaffle and add the other half of the batter to cook the other chaffle.
- Top with your optional ingredients and serve warm!
- Enjoy!

Nutritional Value (per serving):

- Total Fat: 7.8g
- Cholesterol: 111mg
- Sodium: 209.1mg
- Total Carbohydrate: 2.7g
- Sugars: 1.1g
- Protein: 8.8g
- Vitamin A: 106.7μg

Crispy Bagel Chaffle Chips

Servings: 1

Ingredients:

- 3 Tbs Parmesan cheese shredded
- 1 tsp Everything Bagel Seasoning

Instructions:

- Preheat the mini waffle maker.
- Place the Parmesan cheese on the griddle and allow it to bubble. About 3 minutes. Be sure to leave it long enough, or else it won't turn crispy when it cools. Important step!
- Sprinkle the melted cheese with about 1 teaspoon of Everything Bagel Seasoning. Leave the waffle iron open when it cooks!
- Unplug the mini waffle maker and allow it to cool for a few minutes. This will allow the cheese to cool enough to bind together and get crispy.

- After about 2 minutes of it cooling off, it will still be warm.
- Use a mini spatula to peel the warm (but not hot cheese from the mini waffle iron.
- Allow it to cool completely for crispy chips! These chips pack a powerful crunch, which is something I tend to miss on Keto!

Note:

The more cheese you use, the thicker the chips will be. The less cheese you use, the lighter and crispier the chips will be! This technique works well for both textures! Just be sure to use less Everything Bagel seasonings if you use less cheese. You don't want the seasonings to be overpowering to the ratio of cheese you have.

Nutritional Value (per serving):

- Total Fat 5.6g
- Cholesterol 10.8mg
- Sodium 254.7mg
- Total Carbohydrate 1.2g
- Dietary Fiber 0.4g
- Sugars 0.1g
- Protein 6.2g
- Vitamin A 34.3µg

Keto BLT Chaffle Sandwich

Ingredients:

Chaffle bread ingredients:

- 1/2 cup mozzarella shredded
- 1 egg
- 1 tbs green onion diced
- 1/2 tsp Italian seasoning

Sandwich ingredients:

- Bacon pre-cooked
- Lettuce
- Tomato sliced
- 1 tbs mayo

Instructions:

- Preheat the mini waffle maker
- In a small bowl, whip the egg.
- Add the cheese, seasonings, and onion. Mix it until it's well incorporated.

- Place half the batter in the mini waffle maker and cook it for 4 minutes.
- If you want a crunchy bread, add a tsp of shredded cheese to the mini waffle iron for 30 seconds before adding the batter. The extra cheese on the outside creates the best crust!
- After the first chaffle is complete, add the remaining batter to the mini waffle maker and cook it for 4 minutes.
- Add the mayo, bacon, lettuce, and tomato to your sandwich.
- Enjoy!

Keto Lemon Chaffle Recipe

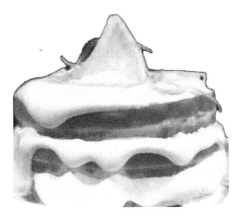

Servings: 4

Ingredients:

Chaffle Cake:

- 2 oz cream cheese room temp and softened
- 2 eggs
- 2 tsp butter melted
- 2 tbs coconut flour
- 1 tsp monk fruit powdered confectioners blend (add more if you like it sweeter)
- 1 tsp baking powder
- 1/2 tsp lemon extract
- 20 drops cake batter extract

Chaffle Frosting:

- 1/2 cup heavy whipping cream
- 1 tbs monk fruit powdered confectioners blend
- 1/4 tsp lemon extract

Instructions:

- Preheat the mini waffle maker
- Add all of the ingredients for the chaffle cake in a blender and mix it until the batter is nice and smooth. This should only take a couple of minutes.
- Use an ice cream scoop and fill the waffle iron with one full scoop of batter. This size of the ice cream scoop is about 3 tablespoons and fits perfectly in the mini waffle maker.
- While the chaffles are cooking, start making the frosting.
- In a medium-size bowl, add the chaffle frosting ingredients.

- Mix the ingredients until the frosting is thick with peaks.
- All the chaffles to completely cool before frosting the cake.
- Optional: Add lemon peel for extra flavor!

Nutritional Value (per serving):

- Total Fat 20.3g
- Cholesterol 146.1mg
- Sodium 93.1mg
- Total Carbohydrate 5.2g
- Dietary Fiber 1.3g
- Sugars 2.2g
- Protein 5.6g
- Vitamin A 222.2µg

Bacon Cheddar Bay Biscuits Chaffle Recipe

Servings: 6

Ingredients:

- 1/2 cup Almond Flour
- 1/4 cup Oat Fiber
- 3 strips of bacon cooked and crumbled
- 1 Egg, beaten
- 1/4 cup Sour Cream
- 1 T Bacon Grease melted
- 1 1/2 T Kerrygold Butter melted
- 1/2 cup Sharp Cheddar Cheese shredded
- 1/2 cup Smoked Gouda Cheese shredded
- 1/4 tsp Swerve Confectioners
- 1/2 tsp Garlic Salt
- 1/2 tsp Onion Powder
- 1/2 T Parsley dried
- 1/2 T Baking Powder
- 1/4 tsp Baking Soda

Instructions:

- Preheat mini waffle maker.
- Mix almond flour, baking powder, baking soda, onion powder, and garlic salt to a bowl and mix using a whisk.
- In another bowl, add the eggs, bacon, sour cream, parsley, bacon grease, melted butter, and cheese. Mix until combined.
- Add the dry ingredients into the wet and mix.
- Scoop 2-3 T of the mix into hot waffle iron and cook for 5-6 minutes.

Nutritional Value (per serving):

- Total Fat 12.5g

- Cholesterol 59.7mg
- Sodium 219.8mg
- Total Carbohydrate 4.3g
- Dietary Fiber 0.6g
- Sugars 0.5g
- Protein 7.7g
- Vitamin A 105µg
- Vitamin C 6.8mg

Lime Pie Chaffle Recipe

Servings: 2

Ingredients:

Key Lime Pie Chaffle Recipe ingredients:

- 1 egg
- 1/4 cup Almond flour
- 2 tsp cream cheese room temp

- 1 tsp powdered sweetener swerve or monk fruit
- 1/2 tsp lime extract or 1 tsp fresh squeezed lime juice
- 1/2 tsp baking powder
- 1/2 tsp lime zest
- Pinch of salt to bring out the flavors

Cream Cheese Lime Frosting Ingredients:

- 4 oz cream cheese softened
- 4 tbs butter
- 2 tsp powdered sweetener swerve or monk fruit
- 1 tsp lime extract
- 1/2 tsp lime zest

Instructions:

- Preheat the mini waffle iron.
- In a blender, add all the chaffle ingredients and blend on high until the mixture is smooth and creamy.
- Cook each chaffle about 3 to 4 minutes until it's golden brown.
- While the chaffles are cooking, make the frosting.
- In a small bowl, combine all the ingredients for the frosting and mix it until it's smooth.
- Allow the chaffles to completely cool before frosting them.

Optional:

Top with whipped cream or the cream cheese frosting. Add a small amount of lime zest for an extra touch!

Nutritional Value (per serving):

- Total Fat 5.7g
- Cholesterol 95.7mg
- Sodium 55.7mg
- Total Carbohydrate 4.9g
- Dietary Fiber 0.6g
- Sugars 0.9g
- Protein 5.5g
- Vitamin A 48.1µg
- Vitamin C 0.4mg

Jicama Hash Brown Chaffle

Servings: 4

Ingredients:

- 1 large jicama root
- 1/2 medium onion minced
- 2 garlic cloves pressed
- 1 cup cheese of choice
- 2 eggs whisked
- Salt and Pepper

Instructions:

- Peel jicama
- Shred in food processor
- Place shredded jicama in a large colander, sprinkle with 1-2 tsp of salt. Mix well and allow to drain.
- Squeeze out as much liquid as possible (very important step)
- Microwave for 5-8 minutes
- Mix all ingredients together
- Sprinkle a little cheese on waffle iron before adding 3 T of the mixture, sprinkle a little more cheese on top of mixture.

Nutritional Value (per serving):

- Total Fat 11.8g
- Cholesterol 121mg
- Sodium 221.8mg
- Total Carbohydrate 5.1g
- Dietary Fiber 1.7g
- Sugars 1.2g
- Protein 10g
- Vitamin A 133.5µg
- Vitamin C 7.3mg

Easy Corndog Chaffle Recipe

Servings: 5

Ingredients:

- 2 eggs
- 1 cup Mexican cheese blend
- 1 tbs almond flour
- 1/2 tsp cornbread extract
- 1/4 tsp salt
- hot dogs with hot dog sticks

Instructions:

- Preheat corndog waffle maker.
- In a small bowl, whip the eggs.
- Add the remaining ingredients except the hotdogs
- Spray the corndog waffle maker with non-stick cooking spray.

- Fill the corndog waffle maker with the batter halfway filled.
- Place a stick in the hot dog.
- Place the hot dog in the batter and slightly press down.
- Spread a small amount of better on top of the hot dog, just enough to fill it.
- Makes about 4 to 5 chaffle corndogs
- Cook the corndog chaffles for about 4 minutes or until golden brown.
- When done, they will easily remove from the corndog waffle maker with a pair of tongs.
- Serve with mustard, mayo, or sugar-free ketchup!

Nutritional Value (per serving):

- Total Fat 5.5g
- Cholesterol 85.6mg
- Sodium 262mg
- Total Carbohydrate 1.8g
- Sugars 0.6g
- Protein 6.8g
- Vitamin A 75.7µg

Sloppy Joe Chaffle Recipe

Ingredients:

Sloppy Joe Ingredients:

- 1 lb ground beef
- 1 tsp onion powder you can substitute for 1/4 cup real onion
- 1 tsp garlic minced
- 3 tbs tomato paste
- 1/2 tsp salt
- 1/4 tsp pepper
- 1 tbs chili powder
- 1 tsp cocoa powder, this is optional but highly recommended! It intensifies the flavor!
- 1/2 cup bone broth beef flavor
- 1 tsp coconut aminos or soy sauce if you prefer
- 1 tsp mustard powder
- 1 tsp Swerve brown or Sukrin golden
- 1/2 tsp paprika

49

Cornbread Chaffle Ingredients:

Makes 2 chaffles

- 1 egg
- 1/2 cup cheddar cheese
- 5 slices jalapeno diced very small (can be pickled or fresh)
- 1 tsp Franks Red Hot Sauce
- 1/4 tsp corn extract optional but tastes like real cornbread!
- Pinch salt

Instructions:

- Cook the ground beef with salt and pepper first.
- Add all the remaining ingredients.
- Allow the mixture to simmer while you make the chaffles.
- Preheat waffle maker.
- In a small bowl, whip the egg.
- Add the remaining ingredients.
- Spray the waffle maker with nonstick cooking spray.
- Divide mixture in half.
- Cook half the mixture for about 4 minutes or until golden brown.
- For a crispy outer crust on the chaffle, add 1 tsp cheese to the waffle maker for 30 seconds before adding the mixture.
- Pour the warm sloppy joe mix onto a hot chaffle.

Tip: you can add diced jalapenos (fresh or pickled) to this basic chaffle recipe and make it a jalapeno cornbread chaffle recipe too!)

Corndog Chaffle Recipe

Ingredients:

- Flax Egg - Mix 1 T ground flaxseed with 3 T water
- 1 1/2 T Melted Butter
- 2 tsp sweetener granulated
- 3 T Almond Flour
- 1/4 tsp Baking Powder
- 1 Egg Yolk
- 2 T heaping Mexican Blend Cheese
- 1 T chopped Pickled Jalapeños
- 15 -20 drops Cornbread Flavoring

- Extra cheese for sprinkling on the waffle maker

Instructions:

- Mix everything together. Let rest for 5 mins.
- Add 1 T of water or HWC if it's too thick.
- Sprinkle shredded cheese on the bottom of the waffle maker.
- Add 1/3 of batter.
- Sprinkle top with more shredded cheese.
- Close waffle iron. Don't press down.
- Remove when the cheese is crisp.

Keto Smores Chaffle

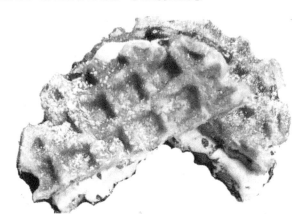

Servings: 2

Ingredients:

- 1 large Egg
- ½ c. Mozzarella cheese shredded

- ½ tsp Vanilla extract
- 2 tbs swerve brown
- ½ tbs Psyllium Husk Powder optional
- ¼ tsp Baking Powder
- Pinch of pink salt
- ¼ Lily's Original Dark Chocolate Bar
- 2 tbs Keto Marshmallow Creme Fluff Recipe

Instructions:

- Make the batch of Keto Marshmallow Creme Fluff.
- Whisk the egg until creamy.
- Add vanilla and Swerve Brown, mix well.
- Mix in the shredded cheese and blend.
- Then add Psyllium Husk Powder, baking powder, and salt.
- Mix until well incorporated, let the batter rest 3-4 minutes.
- Prep/plug in your waffle maker to preheat.
- Spread ½ batter on the waffle maker and cook 3-4 minutes.
- Remove and set on a cooling rack.
- Cook second half of batter same, then remove to cool.
- Once cool, assemble the chaffles with the marshmallow fluff and chocolate:
- Using 2 tbs marshmallow and ¼ bar of Lily's Chocolate.
- Eat as is, or toast for a melty and gooey Smore sandwich!

Nutritional Value (per serving):

- Total Fat 8.1g
- Cholesterol 111.2mg
- Sodium 1352.5mg
- Total Carbohydrate 3.1g
- Dietary Fiber 0.2g
- Sugars 0.7g
- Protein 8.3g
- Vitamin A 94.6µg

Pumpkin Chaffle with Cream Cheese Frosting

Servings: 3

Ingredients:

- 1 egg
- 1/2 cup mozzarella cheese
- 1/2 tsp pumpkin pie spice

- 1 tbs pumpkin solid packed with no sugar added

Optional Cream Cheese Frosting Ingredients:

- 2 tbs cream cheese softened and room temperature
- 2 tbs monk fruit confectioners blend or any of your favorite keto-friendly sweetener
- 1/2 tsp clear vanilla extract

Instructions:

- Preheat the mini waffle maker.
- In a small bowl, whip the egg.
- Add the cheese, pumpkin pie spice, and the pumpkin.
- Mix well.
- Add 1/2 of the mixture to the mini waffle maker and cook it for at least 3 to 4 minutes until it's golden brown.
- While the chaffle is cooking, add all of the cream cheese frosting ingredients in a bowl and mix it until it's smooth and creamy.
- Add the cream cheese frosting to the hot chaffle and serve it immediately.

Nutritional Value (per serving):

- Calories 84
- Total Fat 4.5g
- Cholesterol 71.3mg

- Sodium 122.3mg
- Total Carbohydrate 5.3g
- Dietary Fiber 0.9g
- Sugars 2.1g
- Protein 6.1g
- Vitamin A 298.3µg
- Vitamin C 3.9mg

Keto Vanilla Twinkie Copycat Chaffle Recipe

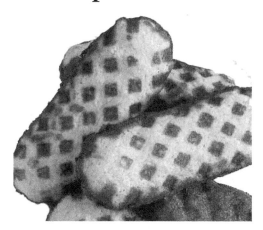

Servings: 4

Ingredients:

- 2 tablespoons butter melted (cooled)
- 2 ounces cream cheese softened
- 2 large eggs room temp
- 1 teaspoon vanilla extract

- 1/2 teaspoon Vanilla Cupcake Extract (optional)
- 1/4 cup Lakanto Confectioners
- Pinch of pink salt
- 1/4 cup almond flour
- 2 tablespoons coconut flour
- 1 teaspoon baking powder

Instructions:

- Preheat the Corndog Maker.
- Melt the butter and let it cool a minute.
- Whisk the eggs into the butter until creamy.
- Add vanilla, extract, sweetener, salt, and then blend well.
- Add Almond flour, coconut flour, and baking powder.
- Blend until well incorporated.
- Add 2 tbsp batter to each well and spread across evenly.
- Close lid, lock, and let cook 4 minutes.
- Remove and cool on a rack.

Nutritional Value (per serving):

- Calories 152
- Total Fat 9g
- Cholesterol 100.7mg
- Sodium 727.7mg
- Total Carbohydrate 6.5g
- Dietary Fiber 1.6g
- Sugars 2.4g
- Protein 6.1g

- Vitamin A 120.2µg

Peppermint Mocha Chaffles with Buttercream Frosting

Servings: 6

Ingredients:

Chaffles:

- 1 egg
- 1 ounce cream cheese at room temperature
- 1 tablespoon melted butter or coconut oil
- 1 tablespoon unsweetened cocoa powder or raw cacao
- 2 tablespoons powdered sweeteners such as Swerve or Lakanto

- 1 tablespoon almond flour
- 2 teaspoons coconut flour
- 1/4 teaspoon baking powder powder
- 1 teaspoon instant coffee granules
- 1/4 teaspoon vanilla extract
- Pinch salt

Filling:

- 2 tablespoons butter at room temperature
- 2-3 tablespoons powdered sweeteners such as Swerve or Lakanto
- 1/4 teaspoon vanilla extract
- 1/8 teaspoon peppermint extract

Optional toppings: sugar-free starlight mints

Instructions:

For the Mocha Chaffles:

- Heat mini Dash waffle iron until thoroughly hot.
- Beat all chaffle ingredients together in a small bowl until smooth.
- Add a heaping 2 tablespoons of batter to waffle iron and cook until done about 4 minutes.
- Repeat to make 3 chaffles. Let cool on wire rack.

For the Buttercream Frosting:

- In a small bowl with a hand mixer, beat the butter and sweetener until smooth.

- Add the heavy cream and vanilla extract and beat at high speed for about 4 minutes, until light and fluffy.
- Spread frosting on each chaffle and garnish with sugar-free starlight mints, if desired.

Nutritional Value (per serving):

- Calories: 96kcal
- Carbohydrates: 3.8g
- Protein: 1.9g
- Fat: 8.9g
- Fiber: 0.6g
- Sugar: 0.5g

Cranberry Swirl Chaffles with Orange Cream Cheese Frosting

Servings: 6

Ingredients:

Cranberry sauce:

- 1/2 cup cranberries fresh or frozen
- 2 Tbsp granulated erythritol
- 1/2 cup water
- 1/2 tsp vanilla extract

Chaffles:

- 1 egg
- 1 ounce cream cheese at room temperature
- 1 Tbsp erythritol blends such as Swerve, Pyure or Lakanto
- 1/2 tsp vanilla extract
- 1 tsp coconut flour
- 1/4 tsp baking powder

Frosting:

- 1 ounce cream cheese at room temperature
- 1 Tbsp butter room temperature
- 1 Tbsp confectioner's sweetener such as Swerve
- 1/8 tsp orange extract OR 2 drops orange essential oil
- A few strands of grated orange zest (optional)

Instructions:

For the cranberry swirl:

- Combine the cranberries, water, and erythritol in a medium saucepan. Bring to a boil, then reduce heat to a gentle simmer.
- Simmer for 10-15 minutes, until the cranberries pop and the sauce thickens.
- Remove from heat and stir in the vanilla extract.
- Mash the berries with the back of a spoon until a chunky sauce forms.
- The sauce will thicken off the heat significantly.

For the chaffles:

- Preheat mini Dash waffle iron until thoroughly hot.
- In a medium bowl, whisk all chaffle ingredients together until well combined.
- Spoon 2 tablespoons of batter into a waffle iron.
- Add 1/2 of the cranberry sauce in little dollops over the batter of each chaffle.
- Close and cook 3-5 minutes, until done. Remove to a wire rack.
- Repeat for the second chaffle.

For the Frosting:

- Mix all ingredients, except orange zest, together until smooth and spread over each chaffle.
- Orange zest (optional).

Nutritional Value (per serving):

- Calories: 70kcal
- Carbohydrates: 4.9g
- Protein: 1.8g
- Fat: 6g
- Fiber: 0.5g
- Sugar: 2.3g

Zucchini Nut Bread Chaffle Recipe

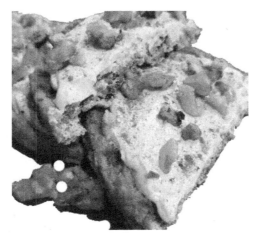

Ingredients

- 1 cup shredded zucchini approximately 1 small zucchini
- 1 egg
- 1/2 teaspoon cinnamon
- 1 Tbsp plus 1 tsp erythritol blend such as Swerve, Pyure or Lakanto

- Dash ground nutmeg
- 2 tsp melted butter
- 1 ounce softened cream cheese
- 2 tsp coconut flour
- 1/2 tsp baking powder
- 3 tablespoons chopped walnuts or pecans

Frosting Ingredients:

- 2 ounces cream cheese at room temperature
- 2 Tbsp butter at room temperature
- 1/4 tsp cinnamon
- 2 Tbsp caramel sugar-free syrup such as Skinny Girl, or 1 Tbsp confectioner's sweetener, such as Swerve plus 1/8 tsp caramel extract
- 1 Tbsp chopped walnuts or pecans

Instructions:

- Grate zucchini and place in a colander over a plate to drain for 15 minutes. With your hands, squeeze out as much moisture as possible.
- Preheat mini Dash waffle iron until thoroughly hot.
- In a medium bowl, whisk all chaffle ingredients together until well combined.
- Spoon a heaping 2 tablespoons of batter into waffle iron, close and cook 3-5 minutes, until done.
- Remove to a wire rack. Repeat 3 times.

Frosting Instructions:

- Mix all ingredients together until smooth and spread over each chaffle.
- Top with additional chopped nuts.

Keto Apple Fritter Chaffles

Servings: 5

Ingredients:

Apple Fritter Filling Ingredients:

- 2 cups diced jicama
- 1/4 cup plus 1 tablespoon Swerve sweetener blend
- 4 tablespoons butter
- 1 teaspoon cinnamon
- 1/8 teaspoon nutmeg
- Dash ground cloves
- 1/2 teaspoon vanilla

- 20 drops Lorann Oils apple flavoring

Chaffle Ingredients:

- 2 eggs
- 1/2 cup grated mozzarella cheese
- 1 tablespoon almond flour
- 1 teaspoon coconut flour
- 1/2 teaspoon baking powder

Glaze Ingredients:

- 1 tablespoon butter
- 2 teaspoons heavy cream
- 3 tablespoons powdered sweetener such as Swerve Confectioners
- 1/4 teaspoon vanilla extract

Instructions:

Keto Apple Fritter Chaffle Filling Instructions:

- Peel the jicama and cut into small dice.
- In a medium skillet over medium-low heat, melt the butter and add the diced jicama and sweetener.
- Let simmer slowly for 10-20 minutes until the jicama is soft, stirring often. Do not use high heat, or the sweetener will caramelize quickly and burn. It should develop a light amber color and will thicken.
- When the jicama is soft, remove from heat and stir in the spices and flavorings.

Keto Apple Fritter Chaffle Instructions:

- Preheat waffle iron until hot.
- In a medium bowl, beat all ingredients except cheese. Stir the jicama mixture into the eggs.
- Place 1 tablespoon grated cheese on that waffle iron.
- Spoon 2 heaping tablespoons of the egg/jicama mixture into the waffle iron and top with another tablespoon cheese.
- Close the waffle maker and cook 5-7 minutes until nicely browned and crunchy.
- Remove to a wire rack.
- Repeat 3-4 times.

Keto Apple Fritter Chaffle Icing Instructions:

- Melt butter in a small saucepan and add the Swerve and heavy cream.
- Simmer over medium heat for 5 minutes or until slightly thickened.
- Stir in vanilla.
- Drizzle the hot icing over the chaffles. It will harden as it cools.

Nutritional Value (per serving):

- Calories 186
- Total Fat 14.3g
- Cholesterol 108.1mg
- Sodium 117.7mg
- Total Carbohydrate 8.5g

- Dietary Fiber 3.4g
- Sugars 1.5g
- Protein 7g
- Vitamin A 148.2μg
- Vitamin C 10.5mg

Monte Cristo Chaffle Crepes Recipe

Servings: 3

Ingredients:

- 1 egg
- 1 T almond flour
- 1/4 tsp vanilla extract
- 1/2 T Swerve Confectioners
- 1 T cream cheese softened
- 1 tsp heavy cream
- Pinch of cinnamon

Instructions:

- Mix all ingredients in a small blender.
- Let batter rest for 5 minutes.
- Pour 1 1/2 Tablespoons of batter in preheated dash griddle.
- Cook 30 seconds.
- Flip with tongs and cook a few more seconds.
- Place 1 slice of cheese, 1 slice of ham and 1 slice of turkey on each crepe.
- If desired, microwave for a few seconds to slightly melt the cheese.
- Roll the crepes with the filling on the inside.
- Serve the filled crepes sprinkled with Swerve Confectioners and drizzled with low carb raspberry jam.

Nutritional Value (per serving):

- Calories 60
- Total Fat 4g   6%
- Cholesterol 67.8mg
- Sodium 39.2mg
- Total Carbohydrate 2.1g
- Dietary Fiber 0.5g
- Sugars 0.9g
- Protein 2.8g
- Vitamin A 45.1μg

Easy Turkey Burger with Halloumi Cheese Chaffle Recipe

Servings 4

Ingredients:

- 1 lb Ground Turkey raw (no need to precook the turkey)
- 8 oz Halloumi shredded
- 1 zucchini medium, shredded
- 2 tbsp Chives chopped
- 1/2 tsp Salt
- 1/4 tsp Pepper

Instructions:

- Add all ingredients to a bowl mix thoroughly together.
- Shape into 8 evenly sized patties
- Preheat mini griddle.

- Cook the patties for 5-7 minutes.

Nutritional Value (per serving):

- Calories 222
- Total Fat 18g
- Cholesterol 50mg
- Sodium 990.9mg
- Total Carbohydrate 0.3g
- Dietary Fiber 0.1g
- Sugars 0g
- Protein 14.2g
- Vitamin A 4.3µg
- Vitamin C 2.2mg

Rice Krispie Treat Chaffle Copycat Recipe

Servings: 2

Ingredients:

Chaffle batter:

- 1 Large Egg room temp
- 2 oz. Cream Cheese softened
- 1/4 tsp Pure Vanilla Extract
- 2 tbs Lakanto Confectioners Sweetener
- 1 oz. Pork Rinds crushed
- 1 tsp Baking Powder

Marshmallow Frosting:

- 1/4 c. Heavy Whipping Cream
- 1/4 tsp Pure Vanilla Extract
- 1 tbs Lakanto Confectioners Sweetener
- 1/2 tsp Xanthan Gum

Instructions:

- Plug in the mini waffle maker to preheat.
- In a medium mixing bowl- Add egg, cream cheese, and vanilla.
- Whisk until blended well.
- Add sweetener, crushed pork rinds, and baking powder.
- Mix until well incorporated.
- Sprinkle extra crushed pork rinds onto waffle maker (optional).
- Then add about 1/4 scoop of batter over, sprinkle a bit more pork rinds.
- Cook 3-4 minutes, then remove and cool on a wire rack.
- Repeat for remaining batter.
- Make the Marshmallow Frosting:

- Whip the HWC, vanilla, and confectioners until thick and fluffy.
- Slowly sprinkle over the xanthan gum and fold until well incorporated.
- Spread frosting over chaffles and cut as desired, then refrigerate until set.
- Enjoy cold or warm slightly in the microwave for 10 seconds.

Nutritional Value (per serving):

- Calories: 334kcal
- Carbohydrates: 24g
- Protein: 13g
- Fat: 29g

Biscuits & Gravy Chaffle Recipe

Servings: 4

Ingredients:

- 2 tbs Unsalted Butter melted
- 2 Large Eggs
- 1 c. Mozzarella Cheese shredded
- 1 tbs Garlic minced
- 10 drops Cornbread Extract optional
- 1/2 tbs Lakanto Confectioners optional
- 1 tbs Almond Flour
- 1/4 tsp Granulated Onion
- 1/4 tsp Granulated Garlic
- 1 tsp Dried Parsley
- 1 tsp Baking Powder
- 1 batch Keto Sausage Biscuits and Gravy Recipe

Instructions:

- Preheat Mini Waffle Maker.
- Melt the butter, let cool.
- Whisk in the eggs, then fold in the shredded cheese.
- Add the rest of ingredients and mix thoroughly.
- Scoop 1/4 of batter onto waffle maker and cook 4 minutes.
- Remove and let cool on wire rack.
- Repeat for the remaining 3 chaffles.

Nutritional Value (per serving):

- Calories: 195kcal
- Carbohydrates: 2g
- Protein: 12g
- Fat: 15g

BBQ Chicken Chaffle

Prep Time: 3 minutes

Cook Time: 8 minutes

Servings: 2

Ingredients:

- 1/3 cup cooked chicken diced
- 1/2 cup shredded cheddar cheese
- 1 tbsp sugar-free bbq sauce
- 1 egg
- 1 tbsp almond flour

Instructions:

- Heat up your Dash mini waffle maker.
- In a small bowl, mix the egg, almond flour, BBQ sauce, diced chicken, and Cheddar Cheese.

- Add 1/2 of the batter into your mini waffle maker and cook for 4 minutes. If they are still a bit uncooked, leave it cooking for another 2 minutes. Then cook the rest of the batter to make a second chaffle.
- Do not open the waffle maker before the 4 minute mark.
- Enjoy alone or dip in BBQ Sauce or ranch dressing!

Nutritional Value (per serving):

- Calories: 205kcal
- Carbohydrates: 2g
- Protein: 18g
- Fat: 14g
- Saturated Fat: 7g
- Cholesterol: 131mg
- Sodium: 224mg
- Potassium: 118mg
- Fiber: 1g
- Sugar: 1g
- Vitamin A: 402IU
- Calcium: 223mg
- Iron: 1mg

Cheddar Chicken and Broccoli Chaffle

Prep Time: 2 minutes

Cook Time: 8 minutes

Servings: 2

Ingredients:

- 1/4 cup cooked diced chicken
- 1/4 cup fresh broccoli chopped
- Shredded Cheddar cheese
- 1 egg
- 1/4 tsp garlic powder

Instructions:

- Heat up your Dash mini waffle maker.
- In a small bowl, mix the egg, garlic powder, and cheddar cheese.
- Add the broccoli and chicken and mix well.

- Add 1/2 of the batter into your mini waffle maker and cook for 4 minutes. If they are still a bit uncooked, leave it cooking for another 2 minutes. Then cook the rest of the batter to make a second chaffle and then cook the third chaffle.
- After cooking, remove from the pan and let sit for 2 minutes.
- Dip in ranch dressing, sour cream, or enjoy alone.

Nutritional Value (per serving):

- Calories: 58kcal
- Carbohydrates: 1g
- Protein: 7g
- Fat: 3g
- Saturated Fat: 1g
- Cholesterol: 94mg
- Sodium: 57mg
- Potassium: 136mg
- Fiber: 1g
- Sugar: 1g
- Vitamin A: 190IU
- Vitamin C: 10mg
- Calcium: 18mg
- Iron: 1mg

Spinach & Artichoke Chicken Chaffle

Prep Time: 3 minutes

Cook Time: 8 minutes

Servings: 2

Ingredients:

- 1/3 cup cooked diced chicken
- 1/3 cup cooked spinach chopped
- 1/3 cup marinated artichokes chopped
- 1/3 cup shredded mozzarella cheese
- 1 ounce softened cream cheese
- 1/4 teaspoon garlic powder
- 1 egg

Instructions:

- Heat up your Dash mini waffle maker.

- In a small bowl, mix the egg, garlic powder, cream cheese, and Mozzarella Cheese.
- Add the spinach, artichoke, and chicken and mix well.
- Add 1/3 of the batter into your mini waffle maker and cook for 4 minutes. If they are still a bit uncooked, leave it cooking for another 2 minutes. Then cook the rest of the batter to make a second chaffle and then cook the third chaffle.
- After cooking, remove from the pan and let sit for 2 minutes.
- Dip in ranch dressing, sour cream, or enjoy alone.

Nutritional Value (per serving):

- Calories: 172kcal
- Carbohydrates: 3g
- Protein: 11g
- Fat: 13g
- Saturated Fat: 6g
- Cholesterol: 46mg
- Sodium: 322mg
- Potassium: 140mg
- Fiber: 1g
- Sugar: 1g
- Vitamin A: 1119IU
- Vitamin C: 8mg
- Calcium: 115mg
- Iron: 1mg

Chickfila Copycat Chaffle Sandwich

Ingredientsip co

Ingredients for the Chicken:

- 1 Chicken Breast
- 4 T of Dill Pickle Juice
- 2 T Parmesan Cheese powdered
- 2 T Pork Rinds ground
- 1 T Flax Seed ground
- Salt and Pepper
- 2 T butter melted

Ingredients for Chaffle Sandwich Bun:

- 1 Egg room temperature
- 1 Cup Mozzarella Cheese shredded
- 3 -5 drops of Stevia Glycerite
- 1/4 tsp Butter Extract

Instructions:

Instructions for the Chicken:

- Pound chicken to 1/2 inch thickness.
- Cut in half and place in zip lock baggie with pickle juice.
- Seal baggie and place in the fridge for 1 hour to overnight.
- Preheat Airfryer for 5 mins at 400*
- In a small shallow bowl, mix together Parmesan cheese, pork rinds, flaxseed, and S&P.
- Remove chicken from the baggie and discard pickle juice.
- Dip chicken in melted butter then in seasoning mix.
- Place parchment paper round in Airfryer basket, brush the paper lightly with oil. (I used coconut)
- Place chicken in preheated Airfryer and cook for 7 mins.
- Flip chicken and Airfry for an additional 7-8 mins.

Instructions for Chaffle Bun:

- Mix everything together in a small bowl. Put 1/4 of the mixture in the preheated mini dash waffle iron. Cook for 4 mins. Remove to a cooling rack. Repeat x3
- Assemble Sandwich's: Place rested chicken on one Chaffle bun, add 3 dill pickle slices. Cover with other buns. Repeat. Enjoy!

Strawberry Shortcake Chaffle

Prep Time: 4 minutes

Cook Time: 12 minutes

Servings: 3

Ingredients:

Strawberry topping Ingredients:

- 3 fresh strawberries
- 1/2 tablespoon granulated swerve

Sweet Chaffle Ingredients:

- 1 tablespoon almond flour
- 1/2 cup mozzarella cheese
- 1 egg
- 1 tablespoon granulated swerve
- 1/4 teaspoon vanilla extract
- Keto Whipped Cream

Instructions:

- Heat up your waffle maker. If you are using a mini waffle maker, this recipe will make 2 chaffles; if using a large waffle maker, this recipe will make 1 large sweet chaffle.
- Rinse and chop up your fresh strawberries. Place the strawberries in a small bowl and add 1/2 tablespoon granulated swerve. Mix the strawberries with the swerve and set aside.
- In a bowl mix the almond flour, egg, mozzarella cheese, granulated swerve and vanilla extract.
- Pour 1/3 of the batter into your mini waffle maker and cook for 3-4 minutes. Then cook another 1/3 of the batter and the rest of the batter to make 3 keto chaffles.
- While your second chaffle is cooking, make your keto whipped cream if you do not have any on hand.
- Assemble your Strawberry Shortcake Chaffle by placing whipped cream and strawberries on top of your sweet chaffle. Then drizzle the juice that will also be in the bowl with the strawberries on top.

Nutritional Value (per serving):

- Calories: 112kcal
- Carbohydrates: 2g
- Protein: 7g

- Fat: 8g
- Saturated Fat: 3g
- Cholesterol: 69mg
- Sodium: 138mg
- Potassium: 53mg
- Fiber: 1g
- Sugar: 1g
- Vitamin A: 205IU
- Vitamin C: 7mg
- Calcium: 107mg
- Iron: 1mg

Chocolate Chaffle Cake

Prep Time: 2 minutes

Cook Time: 8 minutes

Servings: 2

Ingredients:

Chocolate Chaffle Cake Ingredients:

- 2 tablespoons cocoa powder
- 2 tablespoons Swerve granulated sweetener
- 1 egg
- 1 tablespoon heavy whipping cream
- 1 tablespoon almond flour
- 1/4 tsp baking powder
- 1/2 tsp vanilla extract

Cream Cheese Frosting:

- 2 tablespoons cream cheese
- 2 teaspoons swerve confectioners
- 1/8 tsp vanilla extract
- 1 tsp heavy cream

Instructions:

How to Make Chocolate Chaffle Cake:

- In a small bowl, whisk together cocoa powder, swerve, almond flour, and baking powder.
- Add in the vanilla extract and heavy whipping cream and mix well.
- Add in the egg and mix well. Be sure to scrape the sides of the bowl to get all of the ingredients mixed well.
- Let sit for 3-4 minutes while the mini waffle maker heats up.
- Add half of the waffle mixture to the waffle maker and cook for 4 minutes. Then cook the second waffle. While the

second chocolate keto waffle is cooking, make your frosting.

How to Make Cream Cheese Frosting:

- In a small microwave-safe bowl add 2 tablespoons cream cheese. Microwave the cream cheese for 8 seconds to soften the cream cheese.
- Add in heavy whipping cream and vanilla extract and use a small hand mixer to mix well.
- Then add in the confectioners swerve and use the hand mixer to incorporate and fluffy the frosting.

Assembling Keto Chocolate Chaffle cake:

- Place one chocolate chaffle on a plate, top with a layer of frosting. You can spread it with a knife or use a pastry bag and pipe the frosting.
- Put the second chocolate chaffle on top of the frosting layer and then spread or pipe the rest of the frosting on top.

Nutritional Value (per serving):

- Calories: 151kcal
- Carbohydrates: 5g
- Protein: 6g
- Fat: 13g
- Saturated Fat: 6g
- Cholesterol: 111mg
- Sodium: 83mg
- Potassium: 190mg

- Fiber: 2g
- Sugar: 1g
- Vitamin A: 461IU
- Calcium: 67mg
- Iron: 1mg

Keto Birthday Cake Chaffle

Servings: 4

Ingredients:

Chaffle Cake Ingredients:

- 2 eggs
- 1/4 cup almond flour
- 1 tsp coconut flour
- 2 tbsp melted butter
- 2 tbsp cream cheese room temp
- 1 tsp cake batter extract

- 1/2 tsp vanilla extract
- 1/2 tsp baking powder
- 2 tbsp swerve confectioners sweetener or monk fruit
- 1/4 tsp Xanthan powder

Whipped Cream Vanilla Frosting Ingredients:

- 1/2 cup heavy whipping cream
- 2 tbs 2 tbsp swerve confectioners sweetener or monk fruit
- 1/2 tsp vanilla extract

Instructions:

- Preheat the mini waffle maker.
- In a medium-size blender, add all of the chaffle cake ingredients and blend it on high until it's smooth and creamy. Allow the batter to sit for just a minute. It may seem a bit watery, but it will work just fine.
- Add about 2 to 3 tablespoons of batter to your waffle maker and cook it for about 2 to 3 minutes until it's golden brown.
- In a separate bowl, start making the whipped cream vanilla frosting.
- Add all of the ingredients and mix it with a hand mixer until the whipping cream is thick and forms soft peaks.
- Allow the keto birthday cake chaffles to cool completely before frosting your cake. If you frost it too soon, it will melt the frosting.

- Enjoy!

Chocolate Chip Cookie Chaffle Cake

Ingredients:

Ingredients for cake layers:

- 1 T butter melted
- 1 T Golden Monkfruit sweetener
- 1 Egg Yolk
- 1/8 tsp Vanilla Extract
- 1/8 tsp Cake Batter Extract
- 3 T Almond Flour
- 1/8 tsp Baking Powder
- 1 T Chocolate Chips sugar-free

Whipped Cream Frosting Ingredients:

- 1 tsp unflavored gelatin
- 4 tsp Cold Water
- 1 Cup HWC
- 2 T Confectioners Sweetener

Instructions:

Cake Instructions:

- Mix everything together and cook in a mini waffle iron for 4 mins. Repeat for each layer. I chose to make 3.

Whipped Cream Frosting Instructions:

- Place your beaters and your mixing bowl in the freezer for about 15 minutes to allow them to cool.
- In a microwave-safe bowl, sprinkle the gelatin over the cold water. Stir, and allow to "bloom." This takes about 5 minutes.
- Microwave the gelatin mixture for 10 seconds. It will become a liquid. Stir to make sure everything is dissolved.
- In your chilled mixing bowl, begin whipping the cream on a low speed. Add in the confectioner's sugar.
- Move to a higher speed and watch for good peaks to begin to form.
- Once the whipping cream is starting to peak, switch back to a lower speed and slowly drizzle the melted liquid gelatin mixture in. Once it's in, switch back to a higher speed and continue to beat until it's reached stiff peaks.

- Place in piping bags and pipe on your cake.

Keto Italian Cream Chaffle Cake

Servings: 8

Ingredients:

Sweet Chaffle Ingredients:

- 4 oz Cream Cheese softened and room temp
- 4 eggs
- 1 tablespoon melted butter
- 1 teaspoon vanilla extract
- 1/2 teaspoon cinnamon

- 1 tablespoon monk fruit sweetener or your favorite keto-approved sweetener
- 4 tablespoons coconut flour
- 1 tablespoon almond flour
- 1 1/2 teaspoons baking powder
- 1 tbs coconut shredded and unsweetened
- 1 tbsp walnuts chopped

Italian Cream Frosting Ingredients:

- 2 oz cream cheese softened and room temp
- 2 tbs butter room temp
- 2 tbsp monk fruit sweetener or your favorite keto-approved sweetener
- 1/2 teaspoon vanilla

Instructions:

- In a medium-size blender, add the cream cheese, eggs, melted butter, vanilla, sweetener, coconut flour, almond flour, and baking powder. Optional: Add the shredded coconut and walnuts to the mixture or save it for the frosting. Either way is great!
- Blend the ingredients on high until it's smooth and creamy.
- Preheat the mini waffle maker.
- Add the ingredients to the preheated waffle maker.
- Cook for about 2 to 3 minutes until the waffles are done.
- Remove and allow the chaffles to cool.

- In a separate bowl, start to make the frosting by adding all the ingredients together. Stir until it's smooth and creamy.
- Once the chaffles have completely cool, frost the cake.

Nutritional Value (per serving):

- Total Fat 9.7g
- Cholesterol 102.9mg
- Sodium 107.3mg
- Total Carbohydrate 5.5g
- Dietary Fiber 1.3g
- Sugars 1.5g
- Protein 5.3g
- Vitamin A 99µg

Cap'N Crunch Cereal Chaffle Cake

Servings: 2

Ingredients:

- 1 egg
- 2 tablespoons almond flour
- 1/2 teaspoon coconut flour
- 1 tablespoon butter melted
- 1 tablespoon cream cheese room temp
- 20 drops Captain Cereal flavoring
- 1/4 teaspoon vanilla extract
- 1/4 teaspoon baking powder
- 1 tablespoon confectioners sweetener
- 1/8 teaspoon xanthan gum

Instructions:

- Preheat the mini waffle maker.
- Mix or blend all of the ingredients until smooth and creamy. Allow the batter to

rest for a few minutes for the flour to absorb the liquid.
- Add about 2 to 3 tablespoons of batter to your waffle maker and cook it for about 2 1/2 minutes.
- Top with fresh whipped cream

Nutritional Value (per serving):

- Calories 154
- Total Fat 11.2g
- Cholesterol 113.3mg
- Sodium 96.9mg
- Total Carbohydrate 5.9g
- Dietary Fiber 1.7g
- Sugars 2.7g
- Protein 4.6g
- Vitamin A 104μg

Jicama Loaded Baked Potato Chaffle

Servings: 4

Ingredients:

- 1 large jicama root
- 1/2 medium onion minced
- 2 garlic cloves pressed
- 1 cup cheese of choice
- 2 eggs whisked
- Salt and Pepper

Instructions:

- Peel jicama and shred in food processor
- Place shredded jicama in a large colander, sprinkle with 1-2 tsp of salt. Mix well and allow to drain.
- Squeeze out as much liquid as possible (very important step)
- Microwave for 5-8 minutes

- Mix all ingredients together
- Sprinkle a little cheese on waffle iron before adding 3 T of the mixture, sprinkle a little more cheese on top of the mixture
- Cook for 5 minutes. Flip and cook 2 more.
- Top with a dollop of sour cream, bacon pieces, cheese, and chives!

Nutritional Value (per serving):

- Calories 168
- Total Fat 11.8g
- Cholesterol 121mg
- Sodium 221.8mg
- Total Carbohydrate 5.1g
- Dietary Fiber 1.7g
- Sugars 1.2g
- Protein 10g
- Vitamin A 133.5µg
- Vitamin C 7.3mg

German Chocolate Chaffle Cake Recipe

Servings: 4

Ingredients:

German Chocolate Chaffle Cake Ingredients:

- 2 eggs
- 1 tablespoon melted butter
- 1 tablespoon cream cheese softened to room temperature
- 2 tablespoons unsweetened cocoa powder or unsweetened raw cacao powder
- 2 tablespoons almond flour
- 2 teaspoons coconut flour
- 2 tablespoons Pyure granulated sweetener blend
- 1/2 teaspoon baking powder

- 1/2 teaspoon instant coffee granules dissolved in 1 tablespoon hot water
- 1/2 teaspoon vanilla extract
- 2 pinches salt

German Chocolate Chaffle Cake Filling Ingredients:

- 1 egg yolk
- 1/4 cup heavy cream
- 2 tablespoons Pyure granulated sweetener blend
- 1 tablespoon butter
- 1/2 teaspoon caramel or maple extract
- 1/4 cup chopped pecans
- 1/4 cup unsweetened flaked coconut
- 1 teaspoon coconut flour

Instructions:

Chaffle Instructions:

- Preheat mini Dash waffle iron until thoroughly hot.
- In a medium bowl, whisk all ingredients together until well combined.
- Spoon a heaping 2 tablespoons of batter into waffle iron, close and cook 3-5 minutes, until done.
- Remove to a wire rack.
- Repeat 3 times.

Filling Instructions:

- In a small saucepan over medium heat, combine the egg yolk, heavy cream, butter, and sweetener.
- Simmer slowly, constantly stirring for 5 minutes.
- Remove from heat and stir in extract, pecans, flaked coconut, and coconut flour.

Assembly:

Spread one-third of the filling in between each of 2 layers of chaffles and the remaining third on top chaffle and serve.

Nutritional Value (per serving):

- Calories 271
- Total Fat 23.7g
- Cholesterol 174.1mg
- Sodium 1237.2mg
- Total Carbohydrate 8.4g
- Dietary Fiber 2.9g
- Sugars 1.8g
- Protein 7.6g
- Vitamin A 177.6µg

Keto Peanut Butter Chaffle Cake

Servings: 2

Ingredients:

Peanut Butter Chaffle Ingredients:

- 2 Tbs sugar-free Peanut Butter Powder
- 2 Tbs Monkfruit Confectioner's
- 1 egg
- 1/4 Tsp Baking Powder
- 1 Tbs heavy whipping cream
- 1/4 tsp Peanut Butter extract

Peanut Butter Frosting Ingredients:

- 2 Tbs Monkfruit Confectioners
- 1 Tbs butter softened and room temp
- 1 tbs sugar-free natural peanut butter or peanut butter powder
- 2 Tbs Cream Cheese softened and room temp

- 1/4 tsp vanilla

Instructions:

- In a small bowl, whip up the egg.
- Add the remaining ingredients and mix well until the batter is smooth and creamy.
- If you don't have the peanut butter extract, you can skip it. It does add a more intense peanut butter flavor that is absolutely wonderful and makes this extract worth investing in.
- Pour half the batter in a mini waffle maker and cook it for 2 to 3 minutes until it's fully cooked.
- In a separate small bowl, add the sweetener, cream cheese, sugar-free natural peanut butter, and vanilla. Mix the frosting until everything is well incorporated.
- Spread the frosting on the waffle cake after it has completely cooled down to room temperature.
- Or you can pipe the frosting too!
- Or you can heat the frosting and add a 1/2 teaspoon of water to make it a peanut butter glaze you can drizzle on your peanut butter chaffle too!

Nutritional Value (per serving):

- Total Fat 7g
- Cholesterol 97.1mg
- Sodium 64.3mg

- Total Carbohydrate 3.6g
- Dietary Fiber 0.6g
- Sugars 1.8g
- Protein 5.5g
- Vitamin A 52.1µg

Keto Boston Cream Pie Chaffle Cake Recipe

Servings: 4

Ingredients:

Chaffle Cake Ingredients:

- 2 eggs
- 1/4 cup almond flour
- 1 tsp coconut flour
- 2 tbsp melted butter
- 2 tbsp cream cheese room temp

- 20 drops Boston Cream extract
- 1/2 tsp vanilla extract
- 1/2 tsp baking powder
- 2 tbsp swerve confectioners sweetener or monk fruit
- 1/4 tsp Xanthan powder

Custard Ingredients:

- 1/2 cup heavy whipping cream
- 1/2 tsp Vanilla extract
- 1 /2 tbs Swerve confectioners Sweetener
- 2 Egg Yolks
- 1/8 tsp Xanthan Gum

Ganache Ingredients:

- 2 tbs heavy whipping cream
- 2 tbs Unsweetened Baking chocolate bar chopped
- 1 tbs Swerve Confectioners Sweetener

Instructions:

- Preheat the mini waffle iron to make cake chaffles first.
- In a blender, combine all the cake ingredients and blend it on high until it's smooth and creamy. This should only take a couple of minutes.
- On the stovetop, heat the heavy whipping cream to a boil. While it's heating, whisk the egg yolks and Swerve together in a separate small bowl.

- Once the cream is boiling, pour half of it into the egg yolks. Make sure you are whisking it together while you pour in the mixture slowly.
- Pour the egg and cream mixture back into the stovetop pan into the rest of the cream and stir continuously for another 2-3 minutes.
- Take the custard off the heat and whisk in your vanilla & xanthan gum. Then set it aside to cool and thicken.
- Put ingredients for the ganache in a small bowl. Microwave for 20 seconds, stir. Repeat if needed. Careful not to overheat the ganache and burn it. Only do 20 seconds at a time until it's fully melted.
- Serve your Boston Cream Pie Chaffle Cake and Enjoy!

Nutritional Value (per serving):

- Total Fat 53.3g
- Cholesterol 307.5mg
- Sodium 138.3mg
- Total Carbohydrate 10.1g
- Dietary Fiber 3.5g
- Sugars 3.6g
- Protein 12.4g
- Vitamin A 510.8µg
- Vitamin C 0.5mg

Coconut Cream Cake Chaffle Recipe

Servings: 6

Ingredients:

Chaffles:

- 2 eggs
- 1 ounce cream cheese softened to room temperature
- 2 tablespoons finely shredded unsweetened coconut
- 2 tablespoons powdered sweetener blends such as Swerve or Lakanto
- 1 tablespoon melted butter or coconut oil
- 1/2 teaspoon coconut extract
- 1/2 teaspoon vanilla extract

Filling:

- 1/3 cup coconut milk

- 1/3 cup unsweetened almond or cashew milk
- 2 eggs yolks
- 2 tablespoons powdered sweetener blends such as Swerve or Lakanto
- 1/4 teaspoon xanthan gum
- 2 teaspoons butter
- Pinch of salt
- 1/4 cup finely shredded unsweetened coconut

Optional toppings:

- Sugar-free whipped cream
- 1 tablespoon finely shredded unsweetened coconut toasted until lightly brown

Instructions:

For the chaffles:

- Heat mini Dash waffle iron until thoroughly hot.
- Beat all chaffle ingredients together in a small bowl.
- Add a heaping 2 tablespoons batter to waffle iron and cook until golden brown and the waffle iron stops steaming, about 5 minutes.
- Repeat 3 times to make 4 chaffles. You only need 3 for the recipe.

For the filling:

- Heat the coconut and almond milk in a small saucepan over medium-low heat. It should be steaming hot, but not simmering or boiling.

- In a separate bowl, beat the egg yolks together lightly. While whisking the milk constantly, slowly drizzle the egg yolks into the milk.
- Heat, constantly stirring until the mixture thickens slightly. Do not boil. Whisk in the sweetener.
- While constantly whisking, slowly sprinkle in the xanthan gum. Continue to cook for 1 minute.
- Remove from the heat and add the remaining ingredients.
- Pour coconut cream filling into a container, cover the surface with plastic wrap and refrigerate until cool. The plastic wrap prevents a skin from forming on the filling. The mixture will thicken as is cools.

Cake assembly:

- Spread 1/3 of the filling over each of 3 chaffles, stack them together to make a cake
- Top with whipped cream and garnish with toasted coconut.

Nutritional Value (per serving):

- Calories: 157kcal
- Carbohydrates: 5.7g
- Protein: 5.1g
- Fat: 14.1g

- Fiber: 0.7g
- Sugar: 1.4g

Almond Joy Cake Chaffle Recipe

Servings: 6

Ingredients:

Chocolate Chaffles:

- 1 egg
- 1 ounce cream cheese
- 1 tablespoon almond flour
- 1 tablespoon unsweetened cocoa powder
- 1 tablespoon erythritol sweeteners blends such as Swerve, Pyure or Lakanto
- 1/2 teaspoon vanilla extract
- 1/4 teaspoon instant coffee powder

Coconut Filling:

- 1 1/2 teaspoons coconut oil melted
- 1 tablespoon heavy cream
- 1/4 cup unsweetened finely shredded coconut
- 2 ounces cream cheese
- 1 tablespoon confectioner's sweetener such as Swerve
- 1/4 teaspoon vanilla extract
- 14 whole almonds

Instructions:

For the Chaffles:

- Preheat mini Dash waffle iron until thoroughly hot.
- In a medium bowl, whisk all chaffle ingredients together until well combined.
- Pour half of the batter into the waffle iron.
- Close and cook 3-5 minutes, until done. Remove to a wire rack.
- Repeat for the second chaffle.

For the Filling:

- Soften cream to room temperature or warm in the microwave for 10 seconds.
- Add all ingredients to a bowl and mix until smooth and well-combined.

Assembly:

- Spread half the filling on one chaffle and place 7 almonds evenly on top of the filling.
- Repeat with the second chaffle and stack together.

Nutritional Value (per serving):

- Calories: 130kcal
- Carbohydrates: 6.3g
- Protein: 3g Fat: 10.6g
- Fiber: 1g
- Sugar: 3.4g

Pumpkin Chaffle Keto Sugar Cookies Recipe

Ingredients:

Keto Sugar Cookie Ingredients:

- 1 T butter melted
- 1 T Sweetener
- 1 Egg Yolk
- 1/8 tsp Vanilla Extract
- 1/8 tsp Cake Batter Extract
- 3 T Almond Flour
- 1/8 tsp Baking Powder

Icing Ingredients:

- 1 T Confectioners Sweetener
- 1/4 tsp Vanilla Extract
- 1-2 tsp Water

Sprinkles Ingredients:

- 1 T Granular Sweetener mixed with 1 drop of food coloring. Mix well.

Instructions:

- Stir all ingredients together. Let rest for 5 min.
- Stir again.
- Refrigerate for 15 mins.
- Put 1/2 of dough in the pumpkin waffle maker.
- Cook 4 minutes.
- Repeat. Let cool.
- Add icing and sprinkles, if desired.

OREO Cookie Chaffle Recipe

Ingredients:

Chaffle ingredients:

- 1 egg
- 1 tbs black cocoa
- 1 tbs monk fruit confectioners blend or your favorite keto-approved sweetener
- 1/4 tsp baking powder
- 2 tbs cream cheese room temperature and softened
- 1 tbs mayonnaise
- 1/4 tsp instant coffee powder, not liquid
- pinch salt
- 1 tsp vanilla

Frosting ingredients:

- 2 Tbs monk fruit confectioners
- 2 Tbs cream cheese softened and room temp
- 1/4 tsp clear vanilla

Instructions:

- In a small bowl, whip up the egg.
- Add the remaining ingredients and mix well until the batter is smooth and creamy.
- Divide the batter into 3 and pour each in a mini waffle maker and cook it for 2 1/2 to 3 minutes until it's fully cooked.
- In a separate small bowl, add the sweetener, cream cheese, and vanilla. Mix the frosting until everything is well incorporated.
- Spread the frosting on the waffle cake after it has completely cooled down to room temperature.

Maple Iced Soft Gingerbread Cookies Chaffle

Servings: 2

Ingredients:

Chaffles Ingredients:

- 1 egg
- 1 ounce cream cheese softened to room temperature
- 2 teaspoons melted butter
- 1 tablespoon Swerve Brown sweetener
- 1 tablespoon almond flour
- 2 teaspoons coconut flour
- 1/4 teaspoon baking powder
- 3/4 teaspoon ground ginger
- 1/2 teaspoon ground cinnamon
- Generous dash ground nutmeg
- Generous dash ground clove

Icing Ingredients:

- 2 tablespoons powdered sweeteners such as Swerve or Lakanto
- 1 1/2 teaspoons heavy cream
- 1/8 teaspoon maple extract
- Water as needed to thin the frosting

Instructions:

- Heat mini Dash waffle iron until thoroughly hot.
- Beat all chaffle ingredients together in a small bowl until smooth.
- Add a heaping 2 tablespoons of batter to waffle iron and cook until done about 4 minutes.

- Repeat to make 2 chaffles. Let cool on wire rack.

Maple Icing Instructions:

- In a small bowl, whisk together sweetener, heavy cream, and maple extract until smooth.
- Add enough water to thin to a spreadable consistency.
- Spread icing on each chaffle and sprinkle with additional ground cinnamon, if desired.

Nutritional Value (per serving):

- Calories 161
- Total Fat 12.5g
- Cholesterol 117.5mg
- Sodium 86.6mg
- Total Carbohydrate 7.6g
- Dietary Fiber 1.9g
- Sugars 1.3g
- Protein 5.2g
- Vitamin A 116.4µg
- Vitamin C 0.1mg

Conclusion

Before now you were probably asking yourself, "what the heck is a chaffle recipe?" You're now aware that a chaffle is a waffle but made with cheese as the base.

Cheese + Waffle = Chaffle!

You've also learned that it's a great way to eat low carb or keto-friendly foods without sacrificing taste; this includes other stuff you've learned from this guide. I'm elated you've chosen this guide to kick start your Keto Chaffle journey, and I would love you to spread the words too and sing the chaffle recipes all along. I hope you enjoyed reading this book, and it served the purpose for which you bought it!

Happy reading and keep enjoying your yummy recipes!

About the Author

Irma Baker is a dietician and nutritionist. She obtained her certificate from the University of Pittsburgh, Pennsylvania. She's had several years of experience teaching and mentoring people about basic nutrition and diets for an improved lifestyle.

Also, she's taken several courses to boost her portfolio which includes M.S. in Nutrition and Dietetics and several other courses. Her passion includes cooking, writing, teaching, and traveling.

She currently resides in Canada, Ontario and wants to use writing as a medium to reach a vast audience, teaching them about the appropriate dishes and foods to enhance their lifestyles.

Made in the USA
Columbia, SC
10 July 2020